2 THE END OF FORTNITE?

How scary was it when everything was sucked into a black hole and we thought Fortnite might disappear forever? Read all about it!

4 WHAT'S NEW IN CHAPTER 2?

A quick look at all the new features that are a part of Chapter 2, and how you can use them to your advantage!

6 THE NEW ISLAND

Things have changed! We've got a birds-eye view of the new map so you'll always know where you're going!

8 LOCATION, LOCATION, LOCATION!

Want to know the best places to drop, the best places to snipe, the best places to hide, and the best places for Loot Chests? Turn to page 8 and all your questions will be answered!

22 BATTLE ROYALE

All the tricks of the trade revealed – how to make sure you come out on top in every battle you find yourself in!

26 ARMED AND DANGEROUS!

A lot of weapons were vaulted for Chapter 2, but fear not – we've got a guide to the basic weapons that you need to master in order to rule the roost!

28 GONE FISHING

Grab a fishing rod and pull up a chair as we explain this cool new feature, and how you can use it to give yourself a real edge.

30 ROCK THE ROAD

Learn all about another new Discover the best ways to us in one.

32 BUILDING FOR SUCCESS

Building quickly can make the difference between success and failure. We share some top tips on the techniques you'll need!

34 SICK SKINS

We don't just want to win – we want to look good doing it, right? Here's a look at some of our favourite skins in the game.

38 LOOKING YOUR BLINGING BEST

The inside track on Back Bling, Weapon Wraps and generally looking cooler than anyone else on the island.

40 GET YOUR GROOVE ON

Grab your dancing shoes and join us for a look at some of the iconic dances that Fortnite has helped make famous!

42 DEADLY DUOS AND SUPER SQUADS

It's not always every man for himself. We share some sneaky team tactics that can help you and your friends form an awesome duo or squad!

46 CREATIVE MODE CRACKED!

How to build your own environment and create games for you and your friends to enjoy!

MONEY MONEY MONEY

Although there are lots of cool things to spend V-Bucks on in Fortnite, there is nothing you can buy that gives you an advantage, so you don't NEED to spend money. If you do want to blow some V-Bucks on a Battle Pass or some cool extras, always make sure to check with an adult before you go crazy with their credit card!

 ## STAY SAFE ONLINE!

Remember to **always** check with a parent or guardian before adding a stranger on Fortnite or accepting a request.

Little Brother
BOOKS

Published 2020.
Little Brother Books, Ground Floor,
23 Southernhay East, Exeter, Devon. EX1 1QL
Printed in the UK.
books@littlebrotherbooks.co.uk
www.littlebrotherbooks.co.uk
Written by Mike O'Sullivan.

The Little Brother Books trademarks, logos, email and website addresses and the GamesWarrior logo and imprint are sole and exclusive properties of Little Brother Books Limited.

This is an unofficial and independently written book, the inclusion of any logos, images, quotes and references does not imply endorsement. Whilst every care has

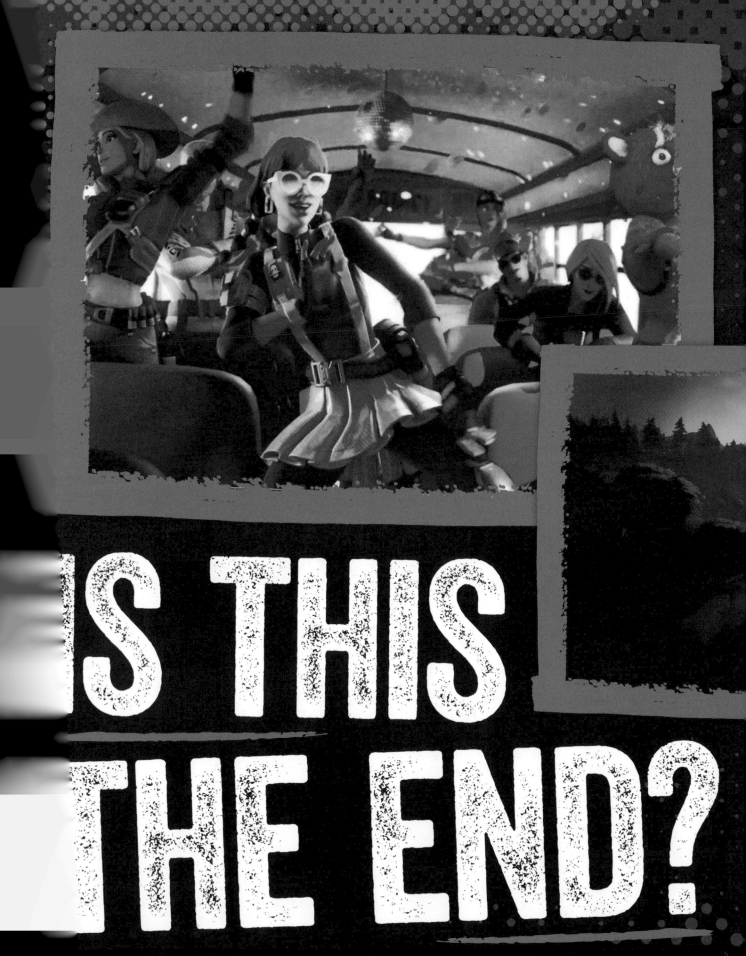

IS THIS THE END?

...was October 13th 2019 when the long-awaited Fortnite live event finally took place, and totally blew the minds of Fortnite fans everywhere!

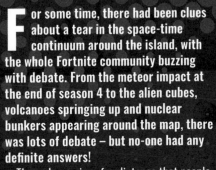

For some time, there had been clues about a tear in the space-time continuum around the island, with the whole Fortnite community buzzing with debate. From the meteor impact at the end of season 4 to the alien cubes, volcanoes springing up and nuclear bunkers appearing around the map, there was lots of debate – but no-one had any definite answers!

Through a series of audiotapes that people found on the map, we knew that The Visitor – some kind of alien creature – was attempting to repair the time-space continuum tear that was happening directly above the island.

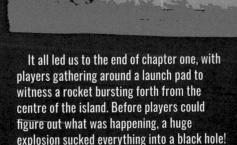

It all led us to the end of chapter one, with players gathering around a launch pad to witness a rocket bursting forth from the centre of the island. Before players could figure out what was happening, a huge explosion sucked everything into a black hole!

For three days straight, the unthinkable happened. There was no Fortnite! Mums and Dads everywhere celebrated, thinking it was all over – but us Fortnite fans new different, right everyone?

After what felt like forever, we finally got our game back – but everything had changed. Loads of things had been sucked into the black hole – weapons, vehicles and more. The very fabric of the island had changed too – a completely new space to explore awaited!

Of course, so much change makes it a great time to get into Fortnite, because everyone is learning the map from scratch again. It means the gap between experienced players and newbies is the smallest it has ever been – so use this guide to help get yourself to the top of the rankings! ✖

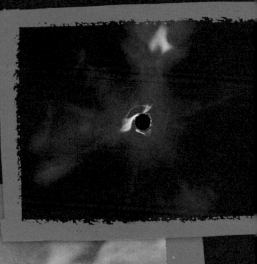

WATER, WATER, EVERYWHERE!

This is the biggest difference! There is now loads more water, with lakes, rivers and ponds everywhere! What's more, you can leap in and have a swim. It can be a useful way to get round the map and sneak up behind opponents but be careful – you can't use your weapons while swimming, so if someone spots you, you'll be a sitting duck (almost literally!)

NEW FOR CHAPTER 2!

After two dark and scary days with **NO FORTNITE** the world breathed a collective sigh of relief when Chapter 2 dropped and we could all get our gaming fix again. But what we found was a very different island! Here's our at-a-glance guide to what's new for Chapter 2!

FROM SHIP TO SHORE!

There are motorboats dotted around the map now – they are the only vehicles available in the game at the start of Chapter 2. There are no other vehicles at all – quadcrashers, ATVs, hoverboards, even shopping trolleys – all gone! However, you can find out more about using the motorboats on page 30!

HOT RODS!

A really cool new feature is fishing! It might sound daft, but you can grab a fishing rod and find extra weapons in the water, as well as catching and eating fish that restore your energy or cause damage to opponents! Check out page 28 for more!

PEEK-A-BOO!

You can now hide inside things like barrels and hay bales, giving the sneaky shooters out there even more chance of surprising their enemies! Just get close to one, hop in, and wait!

BASIC WEAPONS

A lot of the weapons have been vaulted in Chapter 2, leaving a pretty basic selection available. That makes it a little simpler while everyone gets to know the map, but you can bet your bottom dollar that in time, new weapons will be introduced and some old favourites will return!

BETTER BATTLEPASS

One of the changes we're loving is that the battle pass rewards seem a little better, and it's possible to earn enough V-Bucks to save up for the NEXT battle pass too – if you're good enough and have the commitment. It certainly makes things more affordable and fun – the challenges seem a little easier to achieve too.

BRAVE NEW WORLD

After the dramatic black hole event ended, Fortnite players were left with a completely new map, home to thirteen different locations. Only Salty Springs and Retail Row survive from the very first map, and there are lots of new places to explore!

To begin with, the map will be greyed out and as you explore more areas, you'll gain XP and more of the map is revealed. As well as the named areas – which we explore in more detail over the coming pages – there are some landmark areas you can visit to grab loot etc that might be a bit less popular than some of the bigger, named locations.

More are added each season, and older ones stop revealing themselves as 'landmarks' but they are still there – and are often chock full of weapons and goodies just waiting to be found.

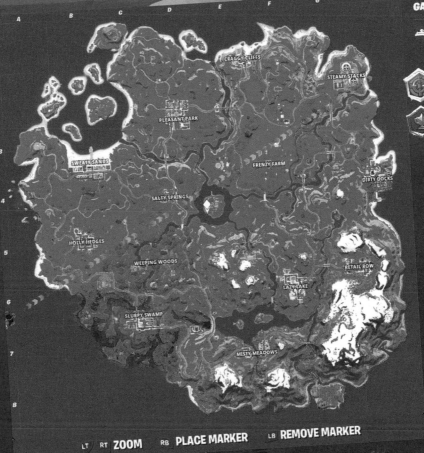

0:03 👤 100 ◎ 0

+8k   +8k   +16k

DAILY CHALLENGES

...ch Chests or Ammo Boxes at Crag
5 / 14

...damage with SMGs to opponents
580 / 1,000

SUGGESTED CHALLENGES

...ive a teammate in different match
0 / 3

...Complete VEX Objectives
3 / 4

...XEV: Finish top 5 in Duos or Squads
0 / 3

...V: Carry a teammate out of the Stor
0 / 1

...XEV: Revive and Reboot a teammate
0 / 2

...V: Assist a teammate with eliminati
1 / 10

...X: Yeet an opponent and deal fall da
0 / 1

...al damage with SMGs, Shotguns, an
0 / 3

LT | RT ZOOM   RB PLACE MARKER   LB REMOVE MARKER

Our list of locations combines a mix of our favourite old and new places on the map, but all are great places to head to if you want to get tooled up without finding yourself in the middle of a huge firefight straight away.

APRES SKI E8	FORT CRUMPET A3	MOWDOWN F2
BASE CAMP HOTEL H7	GHOST HOUSE D5	PRISTINE POINT G1
BASE CAMP GOLF G7	GORGEOUS GORGE F5	RAINBOW RENTALS A6
CAMP COD G8	HILLTOP HOUSE D2	RED STEEL BRIDGE D3
CORAL COVE A2	HOMELY HILLS D1	RISKY REELS E4
CRACKSHOT'S CABIN E5	HYDRO 16 ...... D7	SHANTY TOWN B6
CRASH SITE C2	LAKE CANOE F3	SHIPWRECK COVE H7
EYE LAND E4	LAZY LAKE ISLAND E7	STUMPY RIDGE E6
FLOPPER POND C5	LOCKIE'S LIGHTHOUSE C1	THE ORCHARD F2
FN RADIO E2	MOUNT KAY G7	WEATHER STATION G7

LOCATION, LOCATION, LOCATION!

Knowing the best places to drop, the best places to avoid, and how to get the most out of each area can be the difference between success and failure in Fortnite.

Just as well that our awesome location guide is here to help you then, eh? The following pages will tell you everything you need to know about all the places on the map and even a few sneaky secrets about places that AREN'T on the map. How cool is that! Just don't tell the other Fortnite players, yeah? We don't want to give away those advantages...

TOP 5 PLACES TO DROP

There are strengths and weaknesses to every location on the map, but these are our top 5 places to aim for when you first leave that battle bus. What are yours?

1) SLURPY SWAMP

2) SWEATY SANDS

3) LAZY LAKE

4) FRENZY FARM

5) STEAMY SNACKS

FRENZY FARM

Ideal for the sneaky ones among you! It's possible to hide in the hay bales dotted around the place as well as the cornfields. In the cornfields, you don't need to press the hide button like you do with the hay bales – simply walk a couple of yards into the cornfield, then turn around and aim down your scope. You'll now be hidden within the cornfield, but you'll be able to see out!

It's a great opportunity to conceal yourself with a shotgun or a submachine gun. Wait for unsuspecting opponents to sneak past, then leap out to finish them off before they even know you are there!

The big farmhouse is key to bossing Frenzy Farm. It's a large three-storey building pretty much in the middle of the settlement. It's got a reasonable amount of Loot Chests inside, as well as weapons and ammo that spawn on the floor in there.

If you can get into the farmhouse early on in the game, then not only will you have your pick of the weaponry usually on offer in there, but you'll also have a very defendable space too. You can take the stairs up to the first floor and keep the doors covered, so you'll have the advantage of higher ground should anyone come in looking for those Loot Chests. If you do come under fire and need to retreat, you can go to the back of the landing and up to the second floor, where you can repeat the same trick of defending higher ground.

The bigger bedrooms on the top floor have dual-aspect windows so you can see in two different directions from them – making them a good place to head to if you want to see if anyone is moving in on the farm. There's also a balcony on the top floor that's useful for the same task. For the best views of all though, head up two MORE flights into the split-level attic before removing a bit of the roof to find a vantage point with excellent views..

If you get there too late to take the main farmhouse, then there are several smaller outbuildings dotted around the area that you'll find some loot in, giving you a chance of taking the main house and eliminating anyone in it.

MAP REFERENCE: F4 / **LOOT CHESTS:** ★ ★ ★ ★ ★ / **VANTAGE POINTS:** ★ ★ ★ ★ ★ / **HIDING PLACES:** ★ ★ ★ ★ ★

SLURPY SWAMP

This is a great place to drop – but be aware that makes it crowded from the start and things will get hairy, so you'll need to find a chest quickly and get busy!

Why is it so good? Well, the river of gloop that leaks out of the factory is Fortnite's answer to Willy Wonka's factory. It's not sweeties you'll be swimming in though – it's health-regenerating slime! That's right, if you take damage during a firefight, leap into the slimy water and watch your health increase! If your health is full, then you'll find it's your shield that increases the longer you stay in the gloop. Nice!

The factory itself also provides great

sniping locations on the outside, with the inside areas great for close quarters combat. If you want to hole up somewhere central, the tallest building (the one home to huge vats of slime) has lots of floors, but they are all against the walls – from the top, you can see right down to the bottom which makes it a great place to see anyone coming for you!

Slurpy Swamp is also a good location because it's in a fairly well populated section of the map – Holly Hedges, Weeping Woods and Misty Meadows are all pretty close by, giving you somewhere to move on to quickly if you need more loot, or Slurpy Swamp is just a bit too hectic for you!

GRID REFERENCE: C7 / **LOOT CHESTS:** ★ ★ ★ ★ ★ / **VANTAGE POINTS:** ★ ★ ★ ★ ★ / **HIDING PLACES:** ★ ★ ★ ★ ★

DIRTY DOCKS

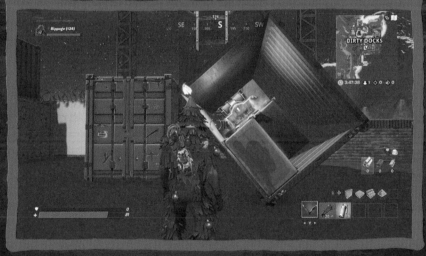

Located on the eastern coast of the new island, Dirty Docks is home to tall cranes that are great for sniping from. The warehouses also offer you a good elevated position to see other players coming from a long way off.

As you'd expect from a busy dockyard, there are plenty of trucks and lorries to be found in the area. Ignore these at your peril! Not only do they often have Loot Chests or weapons inside them, they also make excellent hiding places! Climb into the back, hunker down with an assault rifle or similar, and wait for someone to wander past!

On the same topic, there's an area near to the cranes that is full of shipping containers. It's a fantastic place to hide out in, as there is so much cover – and there's usually loot to be found in there as well.

Once you're confident that there's no-one else around, Dirty Docks is a great place to get harvesting metal. There's not much wood or stone around, but you'll find yourself able to max out your metal supplies in next to no time here!

It can be quite a popular landing location, so be prepared for a few battles early on if you do head here. The coastal location means that if things get a bit much for you, you can always escape via the water – in fact, there are usually three or four motor boats that spawn here at the start of the game, so a quick getaway should be quite easy!

GRID REFERENCE: H4 / LOOT CHESTS: ★ ★ ★ ★ ★
VANTAGE POINTS: ★ ★ ★ ★ ★ / HIDING PLACES: ★ ★ ★ ★ ★

STEAMY STACKS

Fortnite's very own nuclear power plant is home to some nice features, especially if you aim for the cooling towers as you drop in. The fans inside them will blow you upwards so you need to skydive down against the wind they generate, but you'll find a decent amount of Loot Chests when you do make it to the bottom. What's more, those big fans can be a great way to escape from the building if you do get ambushed while you are inside. You'll need to build a ramp in order to get on top of the admin offices inside each tower before the fans will suck you up and away though.

The rooftop area between the two towers is something of a killing field thanks to the walkways that snake around it. They provide plenty of different ways to get through the area, meaning your opponents could be above or below you, so it's not a good idea to cross the central area if you can avoid doing so as there are far too many opportunities to fall into an ambush. The office buildings attached to the towers make good hiding places though, and you'll usually find some weapons in them too.

You need to be careful how you leave Steamy Stacks. If you exit through the car park, don't just head to the exit. It tends to funnel you into an area that's easily monitored by any nearby players, making it easy to be picked off. Instead, break through one of the fence panels so that you exit in a more unpredictable location.

Alternatively, there's a zipwire to the south of the area that you can use to flee if things get a bit too hot to handle! It might not be immediately obvious that it's a zip line as it is a huge electrical substation with a power cable running into it from a nearby tower, but you can use it without worrying that it will fry you!

....

GRID REFERENCE: H2 / **LOOT CHESTS:** ★★★★★ / **VANTAGE POINTS:** ★★★★★ / **HIDING PLACES:** ★★★★★

SWEATY SANDS

A great place to land, this area has chests everywhere. Being by the coast means you have an easy escape if things get too hairy, while also meaning there is less chance of anyone sneaking up on you from behind – you can just focus on what's approaching from inland, for the most part.

The tower to the east of Sweaty Sands is a great place to land if you get there quick – it's one of the highest vantage points in any of the locations, and an ideal sniping den. There are lots of chests on the floors in the tower, so you should be able to bag a sniper rifle quickly if you do land there – the ideal solution would be to boobytrap the top of the stairs and then use the tower near the bar area on the rooftop to snipe in pretty much any direction. If you're not a sniping hotshot, then sit at the top of the stairs and wait for them to come to you!

If you do leave the high tower, there are absolutely loads of chests dotted around the rest of the area too – this is one of the richest areas on the map for loot, so there's plenty to collect. The other hotel and apartment buildings in Sweaty Sands are great for hiding at the top of staircases while you wait for inquisitive opponents to pop their head up...

MAP REFERENCE: B3 / **LOOT CHESTS:** ★ ★ ★ ★ ★
VANTAGE POINTS: ★ ★ ★ ★ ★ / **HIDING PLACES:** ★ ★ ★ ★

CRAGGY CLIFFS

Craggy Cliffs is the northernmost settlement on the map. It's fairly small, but it is home to a few interesting buildings. As it is on the coastline, there's always an easy way out via the sea if required. It's easily defendable too, as the steep cliffs make it hard for anyone to sneak round the back and attack you from the sea (hence the name!)

If you want to get into some indoor scrapping, the large restaurant is the best place to head to, as it provides some decent cover as well as larger open areas that you can keep an eye on as you hunker down and wait.

The majority of the other buildings in the village aren't too great, in our opinion, There are hardly any Loot Chests to be found for a relatively big settlement, and most of the buildings are small, overlooked and only one or two storeys.

There are two good vantage points in the area though. One is the clock tower in the middle of the town – you can break through the ceiling and zig zag a ramp up, smashing the roof panels out for a good snipers position.

Alternatively, there's a three story house to the west that's on a cliff overlooking the village. Get in there and climb up through the roof for views that go on for days.

GRID REFERENCE: E1 / **LOOT CHESTS:** ★ ★ ★ ★ / **VANTAGE POINTS:** ★ ★ ★ ★ / **HIDING PLACES:** ★ ★ ★ ★ ★

MISTY MEADOWS

This cute, Bavarian-looking town has lots of buildings with small rooms, making it a good place for close quarters battle if you are a fan of the shotgun – the assault rifle also makes a trusty companion here. There are plenty of Loot Chests to be found, and there's a huge lake to the north, which makes it had for anyone to sneak up on you – they can't shoot while they are swimming so if you position yourself with your back to the lake and keep checking, you should be absolutely fine.

The town is split into two halves with a bridge connecting them, so be careful if you need to cross that bridge at any point – it can end up being a real choke point in a battle.

To the west you'll find an impressively tall clocktower that's your best bet for sniping. You'll need to build a zig zag ramp up the inside to reach the top, break through the roof and find yourself with great views of the whole area.

As the southernmost location on the map, Misty Meadows is a bit isolated, and its not even on the coastline, so reaching other areas can take a while too, which means it's not always a great place to start from – even though what's there is actually pretty cool!

MAP REFERENCE: E7 / **LOOT CHESTS:** ★★★★★ / **VANTAGE POINTS:** ★★★★★ / **HIDING PLACES:** ★★★★★

LAZY LAKE

This is a shotgun or submachine fan's dream – lots of buildings close together. If you drop here, expect the action to be pretty fast and furious, so find weapons quickly and be ready for things to get frenzied. There are multiple entry points to each house too, so if you sustain damage in the carnage, be careful about where you choose to hole up and apply bandages, medkits and shield potions.

For a pretty small area there are loads of chests too, so arming yourself to the teeth quickly should be quite easy – just be aware that anyone else who landed here will be able to do the same!

The large building in the centre of the area is a car repair garage – there are bouncy tyres on the outside that mean you can easily enter on the first floor if there are opponents already inside. You'll find plenty of toolboxes holding ammunition inside and if you head up from the first floor where the offices are, you can reach the roof. A spot of ramp building later leads you to the very top – an excellent location from which to keep an eye on approaching opponents, and pick them off if you have a sniper rifle.

If things are quiet, you can even head to the west of the settlement for a spot of relaxing fishing – who knows what you'll find!

MAP REFERENCE: F6 / **LOOT CHESTS:** ★ ★ ★ ★ ★ / **VANTAGE POINTS:** ★ ★ ★ ★ ★ / **HIDING PLACES:** ★ ★ ★ ★ ★

HOLLY HEDGES

This is definitely a location to avoid dropping in – and it's not even worth visiting on your way past unless you're being forced there by the storm. There are settlements to the north (Sweaty Sands), east (Weeping Woods) and south (Slurpy Swamp) so you could come under attack from any direction. All those locations are better places to drop in too, as Holly Hedges is home to only a handful of Loot Chests.

The whole layout is also problematic – lots of corners for opponents to hide around, and gaps between houses that will have you running and hoping no-one

picks you off in the process.

You'd think that the hedges would make for excellent hiding places, but you can't run through them like you can with the cornfields, nor can you hide in them like you can with hay bales. They're like concrete walls instead, forcing you to take certain routes through the place. As a result, it's all too easy to find someone lying in wait to greet you with a shotgun blast!

We can safely say Holly Hedges isn't worth even a passing visit. If the storm is closing in and you need to pass through it, we advise skirting around it to be honest.

MAP REFERENCE: B5 / **LOOT CHESTS:** ★ ★ ★ ★ ★

VANTAGE POINTS: ★ ★ ★ ★ ★ / **HIDING PLACES:** ★ ★ ★ ★ ★

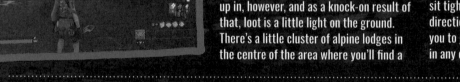

WEEPING WOODS

The best thing going for Weeping Woods is that it's a very central location with access to a river. That means you can grab a motorboat if you need a quick getaway or, if travelling on foot, you can reach Holly Hedges, Salty Springs or Slurpy Swamp pretty quickly and easily.

You'll also find that there are plenty of bushes you can hide in, making stealth a good option should you land here – equip a close range weapon, back into a bush and wait for someone to get too close on their way through!

There aren't too many buildings to hole up in, however, and as a knock-on result of that, loot is a little light on the ground. There's a little cluster of alpine lodges in the centre of the area where you'll find a few Loot Chests. The biggest of these has three storeys and split staircases, so they are useful places to hide out in if that's what you want to do.

All things considered though, there's little about Weeping Woods to keep you there for long – its just a good place to sit tight while you wait to see which direction the storm forms from, enabling you to get to safe ground pretty quickly in any eventuality.

MAP REFERENCE: C5 / LOOT CHESTS: ★ ★ ★ ★ ★ **/ VANTAGE POINTS:** ★ ★ ★ ★ ★ **/ HIDING PLACES:** ★ ★ ★ ★ ★

SALTY SPRINGS

Probably the most central of all the settlements, most of the buildings in Salty Springs are fairly low so there's not much for fans of the sniper rifle. However, it's quite a hilly area and most of the houses are built at the top of an incline, which makes them that little bit easier to defend.

Inside the buildings you'll find small rooms – no huge hallways or lofty landings to be had. That means you can proceed confidently when armed with a shotgun or submachine gun, as you're unlikely to encounter anyone inside who is anything other than practically on top of you.

However, there are some other issues that make it a less than ideal pace. It's

VERY light on Loot Chests and while there's plenty of wood, there's not too much in the way of other resources either (especially metal).

It's well suited to you if you like to play as a sneaky camper, hiding in small rooms and waiting for unsuspecting opponents to blunder in. The central location mans that you'll be able to react quickly to the storm as it closes in, reaching safety quickly, but it also means that there's quite a bit of traffic through the settlement as the storm shifts. That can make it a great place to pick people off as they move through – but in all honesty, we don't recommend staying here for too long.

MAP REFERENCE: D4 / **LOOT CHESTS:** ★ ★ ★ ★ ★

VANTAGE POINTS: ★ ★ ★ ★ ★ / **HIDING PLACES:** ★ ★ ★ ★ ★

PLEASANT PARK

An old Fortnite favourite, but there's a reason why Pleasant Park does not have a whole page to itself – there's not really much to say for it these days. A reasonably central location puts it within striking distance of Salty Springs, Sweaty Sands, Craggy Cliffs and Frenzy Farm, but that's about it as far as advantages go.

Lots of low buildings mean little joy for snipers, and there are hardly any Loot Chests to be found. Factor in the open nature of moving from one house to another, leaving you a prime target for an ambush, there's very little reason to pay a visit here. Unless, of course, the storm forces you there.

MAP REFERENCE: D2 / LOOT CHESTS: ★ ★ ★ ★ ★ / VANTAGE POINTS: ★ ★ ★ ★ ★ / HIDING PLACES: ★ ★ ★ ★ ★

UNDER THE BRIDGE

Our last top tip when it comes to the map is to check under bridges. It's tempting to run straight across them but many of the bigger bridges you encounter (especially the metal ones) will have Loot Chests sitting underneath on a lower platform. You simply have to head down some stairs at the entrance to the bridge to find them. Indeed, these locations can then be a great place to hide – wait until you hear people running over the bridge above you, then pop up and eliminate them!

RETAIL ROW

Another old Fortnite favourite, but another area that's looking a bit sorry for itself now. Most of the buildings are small with big distances between them, and only one real route you can take. That means you're quite likely to run into trouble.

It's also out on its own a bit – there's only really Lazy Lake anywhere nearby, with a hike north to Dirty Docks the nearest location with a decent amount of loot to be plundered.

With very little to be found in the way of loot, perhaps the best thing we can say for Retail Row is that it's often quite a quiet place to start out from – but that's not necessarily a good thing! If you do find yourself there, make a beeline for Nom's, the restaurant, as it offers good cover and open spaces too.

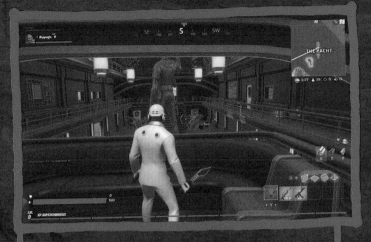

OPERATIVE LAIRS

New for Chapter 2 Season 2 you'll find lairs scattered around the map. These are NOT empty – they're patrolled by henchmen from either Ghost or Shadow. That mans you'll need to battle these bots as well as the other players on the map if you enter these well-defended and fortified areas.

So why bother? The answer is that should you be victorious and overpower the henchmen and their bosses, you'll find yourself with access to vaults with incredibly powerful weapons that can make mincemeat of the other players on the map.

The trick, of course, is not to land in these areas. With no weapons, you'll be easy pickings for the henchmen. Instead, wait until you're packing some serious heat before making your move. If you're a sneaky sort, you'll also find phone boxes near the bases – you can enter them to disguise yourself and get the drop on the henchmen that way instead!

MAP REFERENCE: G6
LOOT CHESTS: ★ ★ ★ ★ ★
VANTAGE POINTS: ★ ★ ★ ★ ★
HIDING PLACES: ★ ★ ★ ★ ★

MAP REFERENCE: C2, G3, B5, D8, F5
LOOT CHESTS: ★ ★ ★ ★ ★
VANTAGE POINTS: ★ ★ ★ ★ ★
HIDING PLACES: ★ ★ ★ ★ ★

BATTLE ROYALE

It's a dog eat dog world in Battle Royale, so we've compiled a selection of our favourite tips to make sure that you are the last man standing! Lock and load!

ONE IN THE CHAMBER

Always make sure that you reload after a firefight so that you have a full magazine! Hole up somewhere quiet and reload before moving on. Otherwise you might run into another opponent only to discover you're down to your last bullet – super annoying!

SWITCHEROO

If you DO run out of ammo during a firefight, it's quicker to switch to the next weapon in your inventory than it is to reload! Put your weapons next to each other in your inventory to save time – when you move to the next weapon it will be in your hands straight away and ready to use!

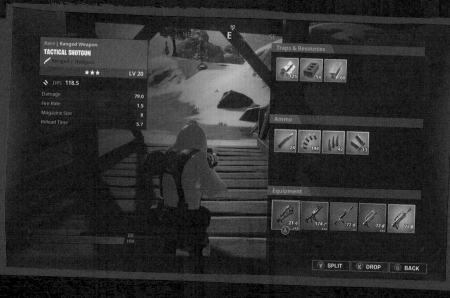

SNEAK A PEEK

Fortnite is a third-person game, which means the camera is behind your character. Use that to your advantage by moving the camera angle so you can look round corners before you actually have to stick your head out. You get far fewer nasty surprises this way!

HOP, SKIP AND JUMP

Moving slowly and in straight lines makes you a sitting target for any sniper looking for easy pickings. Instead, zigzag and throw in the occasional jump – it makes it much harder for anyone to hit you from distance that way!

STAR OF THE SHOW

Check out the status of weapons and be quick to upgrade if you find a better version of a weapon you already have, As well as the colour guide, you can see how many stars a weapon has when its on the floor. The more stars the better – so upgrade what you've got at the first opportunity!

SHHH!

The sound in Fortnite is really important! You can often hear your opponents moving before you can see them, so listen carefully! This is especially true inside buildings, where you can hear people running around on other floors, giving you a vital heads-up that you might be about to come under attack.

SPOT OF DIY

Use the upgrade benches if you've got enough materials! You'll find one in most of the established settlements in the game, and they can help you to improve the status of your weapons!

SLOWLY DOES IT

Switch into a crouch and move slowly inside buildings. It's harder for your opponents to hear you coming that way, and you'll attract much less attention!

GRABBING RESOURCES

Try and harvest early in the game, before the storm forces you too close to the other survivors. Harvesting can be noisy and give your position away, so you're better off doing it when there's more space in the game and less chance of being heard!

SHOT SELECTION

Use the right weapon for the right task! Shotguns and submachine guns will get the job done at close quarters but are much less useful at distance. Similarly, it's crazy to have a sniper rifle equipped when you're inside a building, you might meet someone coming round the corner any second!

PACK CAREFULLY

Try to make sure that you use your inventory wisely and prepare for all eventualities. Keep one slot for shield potions or medkits, and try to have a variety of weapons in your other slots. There's no point in having four shotguns – ideally try to have an assault rifle, a shotgun, an SMG and a sniper rifle – that should keep you safe in most situations!

HEAL THYSELF

Around the map, you'll find ready-made camp fires. You can light these and regenerate your health, stoking them with wood to heal faster. Be careful that the smoke doesn't give your position away though!

DON'T GET GREEDY

Firefights are noisy and will alert others to where you are. If you do win one, DO NOT run straight over to loot your vanquished opponent! Make sure that there's no-one lying in wait for you first!

OPEN DOOR POLICY

If you find an open door, someone's been there first – so proceed with caution! To avoid giving other players the same clue, try to close doors behind you.

LEAVE THEM TO IT

If you encounter two opponents in a battle, stay hidden and wait for one of them to win. The survivor will almost certainly have sustained damage in the fight – that's the time to swoop in and finish them off!

HIDE AND SEEK

Even the bravest soldiers hide. Okay, perhaps they don't – but you should! As well as locations like dumpsters and toilet cubicles, you can also take cover in bushes and cornfields. It's perfect – your opponents can't see you, but you can see them. Wait until they are close and POW!

TIME TO LAY LOW

Remember the aim of Battle Royale is to survive – not get the most kills. Only engage opponents if you have the drop on them and can finish it quickly. Firing at them from miles away will just let them know where you are!

ARMED AND DANGEROUS!

There are lots of different weapons in Fortnite – but using the right one in the right situation can make all the difference. Each weapon comes at different standards – from basic up to epic. Make sure you look at how many stars each gun has as you pick it up – the more the better. Whenever you can trade up for a better weapon, do it! **HAPPY SHOOTING!**

PISTOL

CLOSE RANGE: ★ ★ ★ ★ ★   LONG RANGE: ★ ★ ★ ★ ★   FIRING SPEED: ★ ★ ★ ★ ★

The weakest weapon available – it's better than nothing but it should be the first thing to ditch from your inventory! Can be useful at short range though.

PUMP ACTION SHOTGUN

CLOSE RANGE: ★ ★ ★ ★ ★   LONG RANGE: ★ ★ ★ ★ ★   FIRING SPEED: ★ ★ ★ ★ ★

Causes massive damage at close range, but takes an age to reload so if you don't finish your opponent off with one shot, you could be in trouble! Reload quickly or switch to another weapon to avoid waiting to reload at all!

TACTICAL SHOTGUN

CLOSE RANGE: ★ ★ ★ ★ ★   LONG RANGE: ★ ★ ★ ★ ★   FIRING SPEED: ★ ★ ★ ★ ★

The better shotgun option as it has multiple rounds between reloads. Still causes huge damage at close range, but now you can squeeze off eight shots in quick succession – enough to get rid of pretty much anyone!

SUBMACHINE GUN

CLOSE RANGE: ★ ★ ★ ★ ★   LONG RANGE: ★ ★ ★ ☆ ☆   FIRING SPEED: ★ ★ ★ ★ ★

Great at close range, the rapid rate of fire and reload speed means you can 'spray and pray' and even if you aren't accurate, you'll do some damage! If you're a good shot, it's also useful at mid distance too.

ASSAULT RIFLE

CLOSE RANGE: ★ ★ ★ ★ ☆   LONG RANGE: ★ ★ ★ ★ ☆   FIRING SPEED: ★ ★ ★ ★ ☆

Probably the best weapon overall, the assault rifle can do the business for you both in close quarters combat and at a distance. Be sure to aim down the sight to increase accuracy. Whether you have a burst assault rifle or a single shot, the trick is to keep pulling the trigger until your opponent hits the deck!

GRENADES

CLOSE RANGE: ★ ★ ★ ★ ☆   LONG RANGE: ★ ★ ★ ★ ☆   FIRING SPEED: ★ ★ ★ ★ ★

Grenades can not only be useful to eliminate opponents, they can also flush them out from a hiding place so that you can finish them off with your gun. There's a short delay before they explode, and you can roll them down hills and through gaps – very useful indeed!

ROCKET LAUNCHER

CLOSE RANGE: ★ ★ ☆ ☆ ☆   LONG RANGE: ★ ★ ★ ★ ☆   FIRING SPEED: ★ ★ ★ ★ ★

Using this at close range is not a smart idea – you'll cause yourself as much damage as your opponent! However, it's great at distance and has a big blast radius so you can inflict damage on enemies who have taken cover as well.

HARPOON GUN

CLOSE RANGE: ★ ★ ★ ★ ☆   LONG RANGE: ★ ★ ☆ ☆ ☆   FIRING SPEED: ★ ★ ★ ☆ ☆

Unlikely to get a kill on its own, but you can pull enemies close to you and then finish them off. However, remember that pulling an enemy to close range can also go wrong – BADLY wrong – if you aren't quick to switch to a shotgun or similar!

GONE FISHING

Fishing is a new feature in Fortnite Chapter 2, but it's about more than just relaxing! Grab your cool bag and pull up a collapsible seat – we're going to tell you everything you need to know about making the most of your fishing rod!

FINDING A ROD

You'll find fishing rods all over the map. Often they'll be in a Loot Chest, but you'll also find barrels near the jetties and seaside locations on the map. Sometimes they just spawn on the floor too – so keep an eye out!

FINDING SOME FISH

Look around on the surface of the water until you see circular ripples. Look closer, and you'll see fish leaping out of the water. Congratulations! You just found a fishing hotspot – let's get started!

CASTING YOUR LINE

Equip your fishing rod and aim it at the ripples. You'll see a little arc showing you where your line will land. Press fire to cast your line. As soon as you feel a vibration and hear a splash, press it again to reel in your catch. Then pick up whatever you caught. Simple!

A GUIDE TO WHAT YOU CAN CATCH

THE FLOPPER

Wolfing down one of these bad boys will give your health a boost of +50 – that's more than a pack of bandages. Sadly we haven't found any chips you can enjoy at the same time – maybe that's something for a future update...

THE SMALL FRY

Probably the most common reward for fishing. They will give you 25 health when you eat them, but only if your health is below 75% in the first place.

RUSTY CAN

The booby prize. Throwing one of these at an opponent will cause them a little damage – but why would you bother when there are guns everywhere?

SLURPFISH

The Slurpfish has spent a little too long swimming through the gloopy waters at Slurpy Swamp, but worry not – you can still eat them. In fact, these fish will give you a boost of 50 to either your health OR your shield, making them a very welcome find indeed!

MYTHICAL GOLDFISH

Very rare, but very powerful, these fish aren't for eating. Oh no. Instead, lob it at an opponent and it will kill them – instantly. SWEET!

WEAPONS

Any gun that's available in the game can be found while fishing – it's pot luck what you get so you could be rejoicing with a rocket launcher or gutted to only get a pistol!

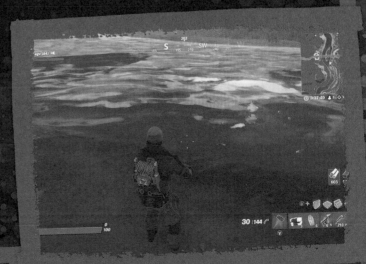

ROCK THE BOAT!

One of the coolest things about Fortnite Chapter 2 is that you can now make use of the water – including leaping into the motorboats dotted around the map. If you're playing duos or squads, they can take up to four at a time. Of course, this is Fortnite so the boats come with a few little extras. Like missiles!

LORD OF THE RINGS

Motorboats are often the basis for challenges or mini games – so far, these have involved leaping through flaming rings and completing time trials. Keep an eye on the challenges list each season; there'll be ways to pick up extra XP points while in the boats!

KICKING THE TYRES

Before you get into a boat, check to see what kind of condition it's in. If it's been used, it might be badly damaged already – check the energy bar before climbing aboard!

LIFE OFF THE OCEAN WAVE

You weren't expecting things to be boring and normal, were you? Good! Unlike real motorboats, the Fortnite vehicles have one super extra advantage – you can drive them on land too! However, be warned – they tend to go quite slowly, and they will slowly take damage while on land – so try not to travel too far.

MISSILES

The boats shoot single missiles, which do a lot of damage to anything – or anyone – they hit. However, you need to be pretty accurate as a rule because they take a while to reload, and motorboats aren't the nippiest of vehicles. If you miss with your first shot, any opponents on foot may well be able to escape by the time you have reloaded and manoeuvred the boat back round to track their movement.

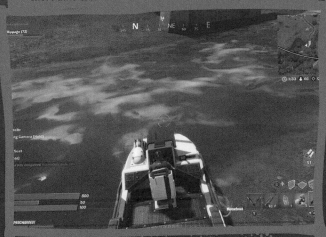

GETTING FROM A TO B

Boats can be a great way to move quickly from one place to another – especially when outrunning the storm, or getting away from a battle you were losing! Using the boost can give them even more speed for a short time too!

KEEP YOUR EYES PEELED

One thing motorboats definitely AREN'T is stealthy. These things make noise. A LOT of noise. That means others will hear you coming or know where you are. As such, don't be too surprised if your arrival isn't exactly unexpected.

BUILD TO WIN!

Building is a really important part of Fortnite. The best players are not just those with the most accurate aim – they are the ones who can use buildings to their advantage. The good news is – we're here to show you how they do it!

BUILDING MATERIALS

It's not complicated. Wood is pretty weak, stone is stronger and metal is best. Wooden structures will be easily destroyed, so you're best off using wood just to reach new areas. Later in the game, when the map is smaller, you'll need metal and stone structures as they will come under attack.

DEFEND THE BASE!

Remember if the bottom of a building is destroyed, it will fall down! If you've built one, make sure the base is well defended – and if you want to eliminate an opponent at the top of a tall building, destroying the base of their tower is a wise move.

REACHING NEW HEIGHTS

The easy thing to do when building – simply put ramps up next to buildings, or use them to climb cliffs you were previously unable to reach. This can help you enter a building on the top floor and come down, taking any opponents in the building by surprise.

DEFENSIVE STRUCTURES

These are something you should build late in the game. Stone or metal walls with a roof over the top (to stop opponents climbing in or throwing grenades in) are the way to go. Once you've got your base ready, pop a window into a wall, and you've got yourself a great little spot to shoot from.

VANTAGE POINT

You can also build a wooden ramp to give yourself a better view of the area around you, to see where opponents are coming from. If you have a sniper rifle, then this can be a great way to pick people off from range. If you're doing this, build double ramps (two wide) to make it harder for a opponent to shoot out the bottom ramp and bring you crashing down to your doom!

TOWERS

Often used in the later stages of a game, these tall structures are just 1x1 squares. Because there are more tiles at the base it is harder to destroy, and by sitting at the top you can see opponents coming, picking them off from distance or at least being ready for them when they reach you.

FAKE OUT YOUR ENEMIES

One nifty trick is to build a structure with a door in it. Leave the door closed, and hide nearby. When opponents turn up and lay siege to the bottom of the building to try and destroy it, you simply step out from your cover and blow them away!

SICK SKINS

REMEMBER THAT THESE COST MONEY, SO CHECK WITH AN ADULT BEFORE YOU START SPLASHING THE CASH!

One of the fun ways of standing out from the crowd in Fortnite is to equip yourself with a cool skin. Here are some of our favourites, to suit every budget – but remember, you don't get any advantages when using a skin, so you can enjoy the game whether you buy some or not!

REY

TYPE: Star Wars // **COST:** 1,500 V-Bucks

Everyone's favourite Jedi came to Fortnite to celebrate the launch of Star Wars: The Rise of Skywalker. She's every bit as cool as you'd imagine her to be! Sadly she doesn't have any Jedi powers, but when you look this cool, who cares?

DJ BOP

TYPE: Legendary // **COST:** 2,000 V-Bucks

What's cooler than a llama? That's right – a llama that's also a DJ! DJ Bop is a bright pink DJ skin wearing what looks like a VR headset. She's part of the twin turntables set, so why not pair her with a glitterball Back Bling while you're at it?

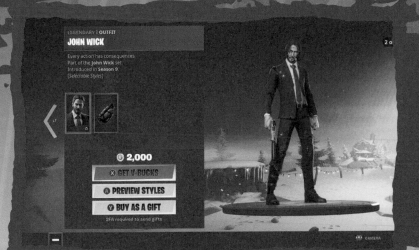

JOHN WICK

TYPE: Legendary // **COST:** 2,000 V-Bucks

The man, the myth, the legend. That's right, John Wick himself is available as a Fortnite skin, so keep an eye out for him popping up in the shop. Just don't mess with his dog, okay? Seriously. You'll regret it

YULE TROOPER

TYPE: Epic // **COST:** 1,500 V-Bucks

Ho ho WHOAH! One look at this fella and the Christmas spirit will disappear pretty quickly! He couldn't be less like the jolly Santa we all know and love – this guy would not be welcome to pop down our chimney. He'll scare your opponents all year round, not just at Christmas!

NARA

RATING: Epic // **COST:** 1,500

Nara is the female version of the Taro skin, and is pretty cool – and maybe just a little scary at the same time. She's part of the storm familiars set, which is based on Japanese spirit animal folklore. The long white horns on the white mask would scare the life out of anyone as you jump out from your hiding place!

8-BALL VS SCRATCH

TYPE: Epic // **COST:** Battle Pass

If you want this cool, black skin, join the cue. CUE! Geddit? 8-Ball was unlockable at level 60 in Chapter 2 Season 1, and his all-black outfit (along with all-black bling) makes him a great choice for anyone who likes to lurk in the shadows...

CRACKABELLA

TYPE: Epic **// COST:** 1,500 V-Bucks

Part of the Nutcracker Suite, there's something just a little bit manic about Crackabella's smile. It's the kind of thing that would keep you awake at night – especially when she leaps out from cover wielding a shotgun...

SPARKPLUG

TYPE: Rare **// COST:** 1,200 V-Bucks

She might look like a mild-mannered mechanic, but this lady will do a lot more than change your tyres and tinker under the bonnet. She's part of the Boneyard set and with so many car wrecks dotted around the island, we think she'll be right at home!

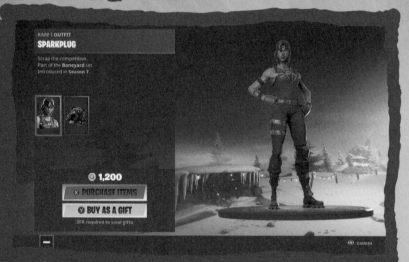

DYNAMO

TYPE: Rare **// COST:** 1,200 V-Bucks

With her cool mask and spandex outfit, Dynamo has leapt straight out of the wrestling ring and into the Fortnite melee! Bright colours, bulging muscles and a completely bonkers look – what's not to love?

SCARLET DEFENDER

TYPE: Uncommon **// COST:** 800 V-Bucks

The beauty in this skin is down to the simplicity of it – the red top paired with the white trousers creates a classic look .

MATCH POINT

TYPE: Uncommon
COST: 800 V-Bucks

Anyone for tennis? This skin is pretty ace, don't you think. See what we did there? The only drawback is that her outfit is so white, she's easier to spot in the undergrowth – so best be quiet and not make a raquet! We'll stop now. Sorry.

MASKED MARAUDER

TYPE: Uncommon
COST: 800 V-Bucks

If you like your skins understated, Masked Marauder keeps it nice and simple – with her backwards cap adding a touch of individuality. She's part of the Banner Brigade set.

COMMANDO

TYPE: Uncommon
COST: 800 V-Bucks

This is a nice simple skin that won't break the bank, but looks pretty cool anyway. We like its authenticity – she looks like the kind of character you'd expect to find in a shooting game. Unlike most of the other crazy skins in this game.

WHIPPLASH

TYPE: Uncommon // **COST:** 800 V-Bucks

This biker chick looks like she's revving her engine and can't wait to get going in Fortnite. A cool split between yellow and black, she's definitely one of the coolest looking Fortnite skins we've seen!

DEFAULT SKINS

TYPE: Common // **COST:** Free

Remember that all the skins you can buy are only really cosmetic – you don't have to spend money on skins if you don't want to! The default skins just rotate through if you haven't bought any skins, and they are still totally cool and fun to play with!

LOOKING YOUR
BLINGING BEST

There's much more than just the skins to help you look cool in Fortnite though! With Back Bling, Weapon Wraps and much more, there are lots of ways to personalise your Fortnite experience. Here's our guide to some of the things you can do – and perhaps some of the ways you can give yourself the teeniest tiniest advantages...

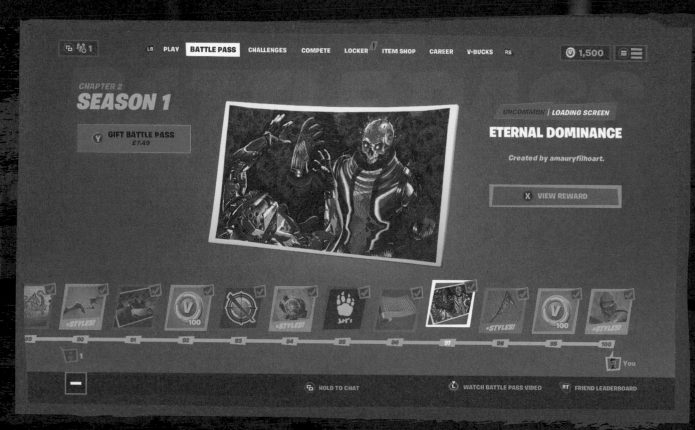

LOOKING GOOD BABY
The first thing to remember is that none of the cosmetic touches can give you a competitive advantage. You don't run faster or shoot better, so you don't NEED to spend V-Bucks in order to look good. If you are on a budget, the most important thing to buy with V-Bucks is a Battle Pass because that will give you lots of rewards as you gain XP – by far the most cost-effective way to get skins and other bling!

CHOOSING YOUR LOOK

Lots of players like to wear skins and bling that they have unlocked via their battle pass. It shows that they are serious players and have been playing a while, and displays their status as serious Fortnite players.

However, some experienced players deliberately shun the unlockable outfits and stick with the default skins. Why? Well, it can trick opponents into thinking they are noobs. When people drop their guard expecting an easy win – BOOM!

COLOUR CO-ORDINATE

There are some bright and garish skins and Back Bling to choose from – but think carefully before you get kitted out! Sometimes, it pays to go with something a little stealthier. Sure, bright pink hair or black and yellow lycra might LOOK cool – but does it give opponents a slightly better chance of seeing you coming? If you are hiding in a bush and don't realise your leg is sticking out, you're much less likely to be spotted!

TRAIL BLAZER

Selecting crazy contrails is another thing to bear in mind! They can look cool, but honestly, our advice is not to bother. Why? Well, if someone has already landed, the contrail makes it much easier for them to see you coming in to land nearby. Turning them off makes you harder to spot. It's stealth vs showing off, really!

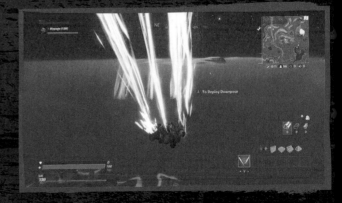

WEAPON WRAPS

You'll gain Weapon Wraps through the Battle Pass system. They don't tend to make as big a difference as skins to how visible you are to your opponents. Some of the brighter ones might be better off avoided, but if you're confident you'll get rid of any opponents who do spot you, then why not go for it and be bold with your colour choices!

GET YOUR GROOVE ON

We all know that it's the totally awesome dance moves in Fortnite that have really taken the game into the mainstream! From the Floss to the Dab with a whole heap of moves in between, however you want to express yourself, there's something for everyone in Fortnite.

The most popular dance of all in Fortnite is almost certainly the Floss. It made its way into the mainstream when Dele Alli celebrated a wicked goal against Manchester United by flossing. The internet nearly went into meltdown and soon everyone was talking about the Fortnite dance moves - even people who had never heard of it before.

The Floss is easy to learn but takes practice to be able to do it quickly – you swing your arms from side to side, alternately placing one hand behind you, then both in front, then the other hand behind on the other side.

Another famous dance to make it into Fortnite is the Dab. This dance started in America but was soon in loads of pop videos, with athletes like Paul Pogba using it to celebrate sporting successes too! It's another easy one to do in real life – just point up with both hands, to one side, with one arm bent and your head in the crook of your elbow. Sweet!

Lots of Fortnite gamers use their dances to celebrate either wining or eliminating an opponent, so it's no surprise that some of them can be a bit cheeky. Our favourite cheeky dance is the 'take your L' dance. It's easy to do –use the finger and thumb of your right hand to make an L, place it against your head, then jump up and own while swinging your legs side to side.

Altogether now – L-O-S-E-R!

OTHER DANCES WE LOVE!

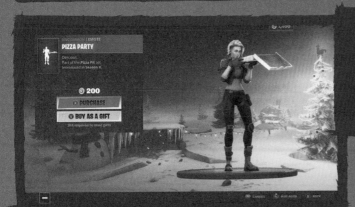

PIZZA PARTY

We love dancing, and we love pizza – so all hail whichever total genius put the two together! Pizza party is a classic – and it's making us hungry.

BOING

Using a llama as a pneumatic drill? Count us in! This one looks as ridiculous as it sounds – perfect!

SLOW CLAP

What better way to let an opponent know they could have done better than with a sarcastic slow clap? We love it – the sheer cheek of it all!

SHARPSHOOTER

Seeing as you probably just gunned them down with no mercy, there's something kinda ironic about using a sharpshooter dance, don't you think? In your FACE, fallen opponent!

SELECTING

EMOTE 4

FILTER - ALL

SEARCH

X EDIT STYLE   **A** SAVE AND EXIT

UNCOMMON | EMOTE

SHARPSHOOTER

Lookin' good out there.
Introduced in **Chapter 2, Season 1**.

(R) TOGGLE FAVORITE   (R) CAMERA   (L) PLAY AGAIN   (B) CANCEL

TEAMWORK MAKES THE DREAM WORK

If you're used to playing Fortnite on your own, playing Squads or Duos makes a big difference! Now, instead of looking out for number one, you need to look out for your team-mate(s) too. Here are some top tips of ways you can work together to beat the rest!

STAY SAFE ONLINE

If you're not in a party, you can join duos or squads and be paired with random players. However, be careful – strangers who play Fortnite are still strangers! If people send you messages or friend requests after playing with you online, then be sure to check with an adult before you accept them. Safety first, Fortnite fans!

STICK TOGETHER!

It's insane not to aim for the same landing area. You might not want to land right next to each other, as you'll be collecting the same loot that way, but make sure you are in the same location to start from at the very least.

If you're playing in squads, you can split into two pairs and head to different locations to get more loot early on, but again, you don't want to be too far from each other so choose adjoining locations.

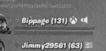

Bippage (131)

Jimmy29561 (63)

Party

244
S   195   210   SW   240   255   W   285   300   NV

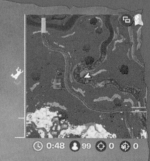

0:48   99   0   0

Jimmy29561

To Deploy Glider

0
100

FLANK OPPONENTS

When we said stick together, we don't mean next to each other! If you're next to each other then a opponent can take you both out quickly. It's best to be a little way apart and, when one of you engages an opponent, the other can sneak round to the side and outflank them!

SACRIFICE

This technique can take a fair bit of trust, but it can be really successful! If you come under fire, one of you can act as a decoy. Run away from the combat zone to lure the opponent or opponents attacking you to give chase. Once they do, the second player breaks cover, sneaks in behind them and opens fire!

SHARE AND SHARE ALIKE

No one likes a greedy team mate! It's best to divide up the loot you find equally so that you both have a decent set of weapons. There's no point in one of you having four epic weapons while the other has a pistol and a fishing rod...

AIM TOGETHER NOW!

If your group encounters another group, the quickest way to get them down is to take them one at a time. That means you all fire on the same enemy. In a duo, you have twice as much chance of hitting them that way – if there are four of you, then that's four times as much chance!

Once the first one is down, you should all move to the second target and so on. This is a quicker way to wipe out another squad or duo than everyone aiming for different enemies.

THE KISS OF LIFE

If one of your team mates gets shot, you can come to the rescue and revive them – but you mustn't rush in! Firstly, you MUST take out whoever got your team mate. You'll need to be quick, as time is limited. If you feel you can get to your fallen comrade in time, build a set of walls around the pair of you as extra protection against anyone who passes through the area, before going for the revive and leaving you both pretty much defenceless!

CALL IT A DAY

Sometimes, the best thing you can do for your team mate is leave them where they fell, and concentrate on getting the win on your own! There's no point in taking huge risks to revive your colleague.

BUILDING FOR SUCCESS

You can build as a team, so make sure you communicate what you're doing. It's best to keep at least one player out of the building enterprise – they should be constantly scouting the perimeter and making absolutely certain that no one sneaks up on your group during the build!

MORE THAN ONE TEAM IN TOWN

You're working as a team, so your opponents will be too! Don't rush in to loot bodies of fallen opponents because their team mate might be waiting for you to do just that. Instead, sit tight – you might even catch an extra kill if their team mate tries to revive them.

LAST MAN STANDING

If you shoot an opponent and he goes down straight away without an option to revive, then you know he was the last man standing in that group or squad. However, that's no guarantee that there isn't someone nearby from a different duo or squad, so you still need to be careful.

ALL ABOARD

If you need to move quickly as a group, then a motorboat can help you do just that. However, it's a big risk to stay in the boat together if you come under fire. If you are shot at while in a boat, you should only ever leave one player in the boat firing missiles. The rest should immediately jump out and fan out, so you can't all be eliminated or take heavy damage from a well placed grenade or rocket.

CREATIVE MODE CRACKED!

> Ok, we all know the Fortnite island is probably the coolest setting for any videogame ever, but one of the other things we love about Fortnite is the creative mode where you can create your own islands, and even your own game modes.

If you come up with something really cool and creative, then you might even find your island featured for other Fortnite fans to play it! How cool is that – imagine how jealous all your friends would be!

So, to help you really get the hang of creative mode, we've put together a list of top tips to creating your own Fortnite paradise!

SEE WHAT ELSE IS OUT THERE!

The first handy thing to do before you roll your sleeves up and get busy creating your own island is to play other people's creations. By seeing games and islands created by the rest of the Fortnite community, you'll start to get a feel for the kind of things you like about created games, and the kind of things you don't. There's no point in spending ages creating a game if you won't enjoy playing it at the end, after all. Start to figure out what you like – games with lots of buildings, creeping around and hiding, or wide open spaces with sniper rifles and long range combat aplenty? ✕

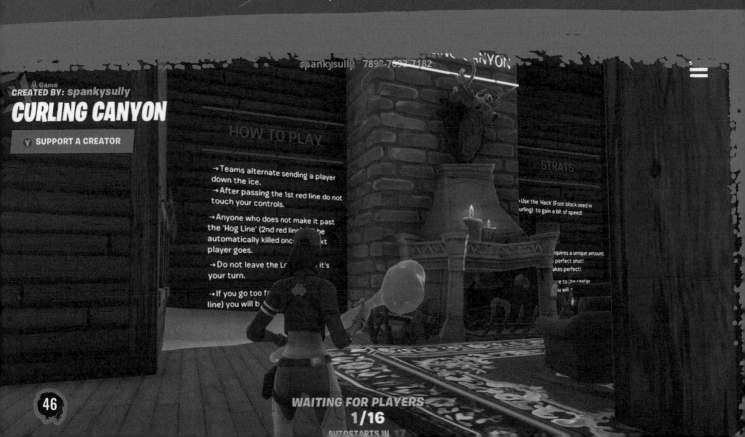

CREATED BY: *spankysully*

CURLING CANYON

Y SUPPORT A CREATOR

spankysully   7892-7093-7182

HOW TO PLAY

→ Teams alternate sending a player down the ice.

→ After passing the 1st red line do not touch your controls.

→ Anyone who does not make it past the 'Hog Line' (2nd red line) will be automatically killed once the next player goes.

→ Do not leave the L____ ___ it's your turn.

→ If you go too f__ line) you will b____

STRATS

• Use the 'Hack' (Foot block used in curling) to gain a bit of speed!

____quires a unique amount ___ perfect shot! ____akes perfect! ____re to the center ____ will ___

WAITING FOR PLAYERS
1/16

LET THE BUILDING BEGIN!

Ready to get started? Time to head to the Fortnite Creative lobby and start your server! You'll find your own personal area with a 'Create New Island' option. You can choose a basic layout, and then it's time to get building!

The first thing to remember is that you only have a certain amount of points you can use to create your island. Everything you can build has a points value – you've got 100,000 points in total to play with. Don't worry though – that's plenty of room to be super creative!

ADDING BUILDINGS

Open your inventory tab and you'll see all the different options available to you – from prefabricated buildings to types of flooring, weapons, vehicles, consumables, the lot! Selecting items will add them to your inventory, and then you choose them in the same way you would a weapon. If you select a building, then you can throw it as if it was a grenade. Instead of an explosion, a whole building will appear wherever you aimed!

ADDING WEAPONS

Now you've got your structures in place, it's time to make sure visitors to your island have some weapons to have fun with! You'll find weapons to the right of the inventory, and you'll be able to select any weapons you like – even vaulted ones. You can spawn them on your island individually, or add them to chests or llamas (you can have up to 50 inside a chest!).

You'll also need ammunition, so don't forget to leave that dotted around the place too, along with other consumables like grenades and shield potions.

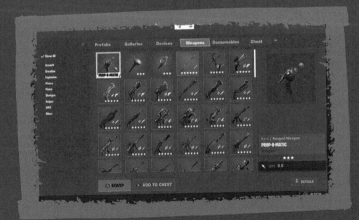

HOW CAN I INVITE MY FRIENDS TO MY ISLAND?

Firstly, you'll need to set up a party for you and all your friends. Then head into a lobby in creative mode and your friends will join you – you can then enter an island of your own making by selecting it from a list of islands you have already created, or make a new one!

MAKING YOUR OWN GAME

Head to the inventory screen and move to the 'My Island' menu. This is where you can really start to personalise the experience. You can choose whether your game is going to be team-based or a free-for-all. You can decide how much health and shield players start with, whether they can have infinite ammunition, and how much damage pickaxes can do to buildings (if any – you can make buildings invincible if you want!).

You can also choose whether players will take damage if they fall, whether or not items will be dropped when a player is eliminated, and who can see player names and where they are on the map – everyone, or your team mates.

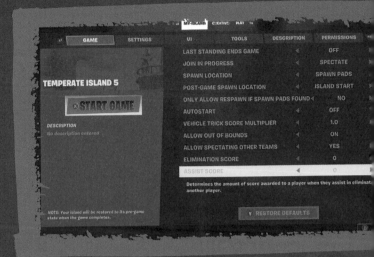

STARTING AGAIN

Sometimes you want to just rip it all up and start from scratch again! If that happens to you, not many people know that you can delete everything on your island in one move. Deleting it all item by item can take ages!

To do this, select 'My Island' from the in-game menu (while you're exploring your island) and then select 'Island Tools'. In there, you'll find the 'Reset Island' option. Everything will disappear and you can start again – saving time and hassle!

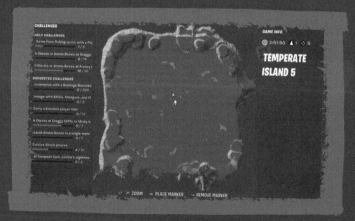

GETTING IT PUBLISHED

If you'd like your island to be shared with the community, you'll need to head to Epic's website and fill in an online form. To earn money from your creation, you'll need to meet very specific guidelines, including having over 1,000 followers on social media.

The other route is to fill in a creative content submission. Someone from Epic will look at your island and might allow it to be shared with the Fortnite community. However, you should know that Epic get thousands of requests like this, so the chances of being chosen are very small. Still, it never hurts to ask though!

GETTING CREATIVE!

Ok, so now you know how to create your own island – but how about some inspiration for some types of game to play? Here are a few suggestions from us about games you could create – why not get together with your friends and give them a go? What game styles can you create?

PICKAXE PARTY

Create your island, but don't put ANY weapons on the map. Instead, all of the players can only cause damage using their pickaxes! Get ready for some serious hand-to-hand combat!

PISTOLS ONLY

This is a game mode that has proven popular in lots of shooter games. The only weapons allowed on the the the map are pistols. With no rifles, shotguns or sniper rifles to be found, it can make for a fast and frantic game!

SNIPERS ONLY

This is probably the opposite of the pickaxe party idea! By only permitting sniper rifles, you'll ensure people are left trying to pick each other off from distance. If you build an island with lots of cover, sniping vantage points and bushes to hide in, you can turn this into an incredibly edgy gaming experience!

PARKOUR PERFECTION

In the prefabs section of the inventory, you'll find a parkour section. You can add some really cool parkour elements to your map to make a course of your own. Then invite your mates to your party and see who can race around it the quickest – or pull off the sickest stunts!

RACE YOUR FRIENDS!

Spend some time turning your island into a massive racetrack using the galleries pieces. Once you've got a course laid out, spawn some quadcrushers and invite your friends to your party. Jump on a quadcrusher each and race around your island – you can add traps on the corners if anyone runs wide as an extra bit of excitement!

HUNT THE LONE WOLF

By setting the team size to 'Dynamic' in the 'Game' tab under 'My Island', you can set up games where one player is on their own. The others then have to work together to find and eliminate the lone wolf – while the lone wolf will need to be extremely sneaky to stay alive for a while!